T0129697

# POEMS OF *Faith* IN THE *Garden* OF HOPE & GRACE

TRACY MATARAZZO

WESTBOW
PRESS®
A DIVISION OF THOMAS NELSON
& ZONDERVAN

WestBow Press books may be ordered through booksellers or by contacting:

WestBow Press
A Division of Thomas Nelson & Zondervan
1663 Liberty Drive
Bloomington, IN 47403
www.westbowpress.com
1 (866) 928-1240

ISBN: 978-1-9736-8753-5 (sc)
ISBN: 978-1-9736-8754-2 (e)

Library of Congress Control Number: 2020904055

Print information available on the last page.

WestBow Press rev. date: 03/12/2020

For God—because each poem came from Him, inspired by His Holy Spirit, to be written down.

For anyone whom God has determined to read these poems—to increase in wisdom and knowledge.

And last but not least, for my husband, Lou, for being a constant force of strength and support, and my loving children, who made my life worth living!

# Contents

# Genesis

God slowly moves the morning mist.
It gently rises from where it sits.

The breezes blow;
The flowers grow.
The honeybees sow,
And nature goes the way God intended it.

Man and woman tend the garden
East in Eden,

Where joy is partaken
From morning till evening,
Enjoying the comfort of God's provision
In the land that He envisioned.

September 25, 2012

# Frozen in PTSD

The sun's coming out from behind the clouds,
coming out—like me,
coming out from dark memories of the past.
My legs stretch out to the steel green deck table,
my clogs resting on its metal as the chair firmly holds me there.
I set my gaze upon a tree;
its arms of brown open their fingers of green.
It is not yet summer,
so they're still hanging on to their helicoptered seeds.
I consciously breathe air in, air out,
d-e-e-p-l-y in, d-e-e-p-l-y out.
Smells of charcoal-grilled hamburger fill my nose.
I swirl bubbly, warm Diet Coke in my mouth,
the carbonation of bubbles erupting from the can.
All my senses anchor me in the present, alerting me to who I am.

I thank my God for moving me through this panic-stricken moment.
I know the seasons will turn, and spring flowers will bloom
once again, and everything will continue growing and changing,
as will I.
I'm grounded now in the chair on my back deck
as the world comes into focus, God making me aware I will be okay.
I can move forward with His leading, even when I suffer disparaging feelings.

When the world closes in on you—
wait, and pray ...
wait, and pray ...
wait, and pray ...
He'll clear the way.
Then take one step ... move forward ... don't be afraid.
Jesus speaks: "I am with you always, even to the end of the age" (Matthew 28:20).
It is He who, at these times (and time and time again), helps me on my way.

May 09, 2019

# Beyond All Else

I am
very mindful
of the brokenness
of this world,
indebted to
Jesus and His burst into history.

Grateful
beyond all else
for His amazing grace and mercy,
aware
of Christ's perfect peace
offered to our imperfect, fractured world.

Walking
in His Spirit
with my whole being,
waiting and watching,
anticipating His return in the clouds
or meeting Him face to face in death!

December 08, 2018

# God Offered His Hand

My own sin did me in; it put me in a tailspin.
I took my eyes off the Lord, and I sank down more and more.
Into despair I went; couldn't lift my head to catch my breath.
I thought I was going crazy. "I'm certainly not lazy," I said.

I kept myself busy trying worldly solutions,
But today, I realized it was mind pollution.
Not leaning on God as I always do,
Not relying on prayer to stay strong and true.

So I leaned on Him and prayed like this:
"Help me stop and not run. I know that's not where peace
comes from. It comes from You and You alone. You're the
answer, my all in one."

So every day, I take His hand, and when I ask, He makes
known His plan:
"Just call to Me" (Jeremiah 33:3). And He tells me things I
cannot see. When I ask in belief, His knowledge is given; when
I ask for His wisdom, I receive 'cause I've listened!

Thank You, God, for holding my hand
When I'm over my head and cannot stand.
Thank You, Lord, for having me land
On the rock of ages when I'm sinking again.


Amen.

July 08, 2018

# Listen

There's a time
to be born
and a time to
die (Ecclesiastes 3:2),
and only God knows when,
and only God knows why.

It's God we can trust;
He won't lead us astray.
For all paths
before us,
He'll lead
the right way.

Trust Him now;
He will show us somehow.
The path's bright
it's not dim,
our future is
with Him.

January 07, 2019

# Jesus—The Glory of God

No one can stare at the sun
when the breeze blows the clouds away (Job 37:21),
just as God's splendor—
Royal! Majestic! Penetrating! Glorious! Too bright to behold.

Moses had to be covered by God's hand—
the tabernacle curtains erected
to shield the Israelites from His destroying brilliance.
Not until Jesus came—then

eyes saw Him,
ears heard Him,
hands touched Him.

They could look upon Messiah Savior; yet
within His earthly body, Jesus was still
Royal! Majestic! The penetrating glory of the Creator!

## —God—

February 02, 2019

# Deliverance

I drew nigh to God, and He drew nigh to me.
I didn't cry or beg or issue eternal pleas.
I called to Him in trusting faith,
And the Spirit didn't make me wait.
In kindness and patience, I was certainly aware.
He delivered me from all dread and despair.

I could not, in words, describe
The peace and comfort He did provide
As I met with doctors one by one,
Thinking my life was truly done.
In kindness and patience, delivered from all despair—
In kindness and patience, I was truly aware.

In my anxious heart, He swept each doubt away,
Asking many questions, Him answering as I prayed.
Understanding life is hard, persevering all the way,
Running the race, until the final day.
In kindness and patience, I'm always aware
He's continued to deliver me from my dread and despair.

February 18, 2019

# Free Will

I imagine
the worst pain God feels
is when His children walk away
silently,
turning their backs on Him
without as much as a goodbye.

I imagine
the burden to His heart
when from the start, He knew
Adam and Eve,
His creation,
given free will, would disobey.

He foreknew
mankind's suffering and pain,
and the plan to return
was established
long before His creation of
beast and man.

April 02, 2019

# God's Delay

I get carried away
with my plans for today,
but God may deliver a type
of delay.

So, in my life,
I'm instructed to pray,
while the Lord will say,
*"No need for dismay"* (Isaiah 41:10).

How should I pray?
I thank You in all circumstances,
for this is God's will in Christ Jesus (1 Thessalonians 5:18).

And I pray also,
"Lord, give me what I need today
and for each and every
untimely delay.
Amen."

May 23, 2019

# In a Blink of an Eye

Forbidden fruit in the garden—
God's ultimate test,
a command that was given,
the test not been passed.

Sacrifice on Calvary's hill
had always been God's plan
through the seed of the woman,
Moses, Abraham.

Our battle won,
God's kingdom will come.
Messiah's last breath speaking,
*"It is finished"* (John 19:30). It's done.

Between Genesis and now,
time is determined somehow.
How God sees fit—
we're all waiting for it—Christ's return.
"Yes, Lord!" we cry; we're all waiting for it.

Jesus arrives in a blink of an eye
with a heavenly shout at the last trumpet blast.
Earth's corruption has ended
forever—at last.

June 05, 2019

# A Time, a Purpose, a Reason

It's not my decision to make.
My life is not something to take.
I was born for a reason,
A time, and a season,
And a purpose,
And a lot is at stake!

Don't mean to cause so much pain;
Seems I do it again and again.
So many mistakes,
But whatever it takes,
Give my struggles to Him
When life's bright, when it's dim!

Praying so hard for us too,
Praying He'd step in and renew
Strength and comfort
For me and for you.
Now good for each other, God knew.
Finally, good for our children—that too!

July 08, 2019

# Pain, Pain, Go Away

I cannot understand, Lord,
Why You allow such pain,
Why it's allowed to stay,
Why You don't take it away.
You can make it go
Like a bird in flight.
What am I doing wrong?
Teach me to live right.
I know I'm not to question
Your will—eternal, supreme.
And I heard from You, regarding it,
*"Be still and come to Me"* (Psalm 46:10).
*"Be still and trust in Me"* (Jeremiah 17:7).
I've learned in trying moments
Over the span of many years,
Yet emotional and/or physical pain
Triggers always awful fear.
Yet I know deep in my spirit,
You desire me to let pain go,
To know You'll hold me safely,
To walk through life, we'll always go.

July 04, 2019

# Keep Watch!

You won't see God's glory
If blind or asleep;
Satan's placed most in slumber.
They're down gravely deep.

Some experience joy;
Others hopelessly weep,
So encourage one another.
Help the ones who are weak.

In our apocalyptic times,
all people pay mind.
God will complete His plan
With sickle at hand.

At the very last hour,
Christ will yield His great power.
In one righteous, fell sweep,
The angel collects harvest wheat.

So blessed are the ones
Who've stayed fully awake,
Watching and waiting on earth,
Knowing eternity's at stake.

They're all righteously clothed,
Wholly ready to go,
And are not shamefully or shockingly
Or nakedly exposed.

July 05, 2019

# Heavenward

What should I do with all my cares?
They're offered heavenward with all my prayers.
You know my heart with all my fears,
And Your open hand catch fallen tears.
Why so much pain throughout the years?
It always catches us unaware.
"Till death do part"
Were vows we took,
But this medical news really shook
The promise of living
Healthy and strong.
Was this Your plan all along?

July 13, 2019

# Alpha and Omega

"It's the beginning of the end," the world naively says. But God
designed this life, dear friends, for He's the beginning and the end.

When you feel inside, you're upside down,
Change your focus to the crown:
Christ's crown of glory, the crown of gold.
He's above all earthly things, you know.
And fix your eyes on things above,
And love as Jesus taught to love.

    Oh, dear Father on holy hill,
    Holy is Your name; it's holy still.
    The great universe stands
    Since time began,
    Your will accomplished
    As You've planned.
    You've so many promises,
    Giving us what we need,
    Just as You've written
    And guaranteed.
    Help us know sin's cast away,
    Remembered no more
    On any day.
    And Messiah, you will help us grow
    Each day in knowledge
    So we will know
    That since our birth,
    Since time's begun,
    You've fought our battles,
    And we have won!

He was in the beginning, and He is the end. It's always been that way, my friends!

Thank You, Jesus. Thank You. Amen.

July 14, 2019

# God's Perfect Plan

The God of ancient days
Had always a master plan.
He worked our whole lives out
So we can take our stand

Against the fiercest storms,
Against trials great and small.
When heavy burdens fell,
We stand and stood them all.

God is the great I Am.
Some today don't understand.
He designed life all with patience
And always had a plan.

He's coming back someday,
Though when I cannot say.
But rest assured of this date—
It won't be early.

It won't be late!

July 21, 2019

# *Diamonds for His Kingdom*

*Observing the Housatonic River from the third-floor waiting area,*
*I watch the waters gently flowing;*
*riverbank trees are overgrowing.*

*The ripples of water reflect sunshine as diamonds do,*
*and at the river's edge, the current*
*sparkles brighter too.*
*Did ya ever notice the river glistening brightest at the water's edge?*

*In the same way, the Lord illuminates my path so I can see clear.*
*He is always so close and always so near.*
*That's how my Savior works.*

*Jesus guides me down a path like that river,*
*Always flowing forward, sometimes swiftly turning, at times gently churning,*
*and He shines light in my life where it's dark.*
*Like a brilliant diamond, He calls me out.*

*I follow Him as He directs me in my life*
*through twists and turns.*
*I'm rough around the edges; yet He continues to*
*change me into a diamond.*

*Who knew?*
*Like us all,*
*diamonds for His kingdom.*

*July 24, 2019*

# Grief

*Grief in life has many stages.*
*It's been that way throughout the ages.*
*Waves of sadness come and go;*
*It comes in strong like silent rolls.*
*In and over*
*And back it goes,*
*In and out—*
*No one knows.*

*You walk through grief, its many stages.*
*Anger wells up in silent rages.*
*It rips you up*
*And tears you down.*
*You smile for others*
*When they're around.*

*Then one day, grief doesn't stay.*
*It flies somewhere far, far away.*
*The light shines through; acceptance comes,*
*And you don't know how or where it's from.*
*But you have no strength to really care*
*When people kindly ask to share*

> *Your denial,*
>> *Your anger,*
>>> *Your bargaining—if only—*
>>>> *Your depression,*
>>>>> *Your acceptance.*

*'Cause then, grief rolls back in again …*

*August 06, 2019*

# Inheritance

There's a place for us in heaven.

We're sealed with God's Spirit.

There's a place for us

On heaven's streets,

Though not by our own merit.

Christ promised sweet inheritance,

Inheritance in heaven.

Waiting there to call us home,

He's seated on His priestly throne.

So keep the faith, and keep the hope.

We're sealed with God's Spirit.

Our inheritance, it waits for us

Through death on earth—don't fear it.

August 09, 2019

# Stand until the End

Stand your ground,
And don't back down.
Look around;
Satan's tactics abound.
Don't be fooled—
He's not worried 'bout you.
Don't be fooled.
He don't care about you!

Shout, "Back off, Satan!
And stop lying too!
I am listening to God!
I'm not listening to you!
Move out of my way!
I won't have you today!
You tempt me to come!
I'm not going to stay!"

Stand your ground,
And don't back down.
Be smart and aware;
He's lurking out there.
Be smart; have no fear.
He doesn't at all care.
Draw nigh to God.
Resist Satan, and say,

"God's given me His power,
And it's in me to stay!"

August 11, 2019

# Restoration

Lucifer was thrown out of heaven. To earth, he was thrown
For desiring God's power and to sit on His throne.

Satan's sin altered our blissful paradise story.
He grinned when Eve listened, facing pain to his glory.

His plan was to kill, to steal and destroy,
Our tie to the Father and all of our joy.

Observe Satan's schemes; see them all crystal clear.
His tactics are hellish; his weapon is fear.

But remember God's purpose: life eternal in heaven.
And our prayers that we pray are our spiritual weapons.

Humanity's restoration is clearly confirmed,
And Christ daily whispers to stand fast and firm.

Restoration happened countless years ago.
Satan doesn't keep steeling what he originally stole.

God ended his plan—finished it long, long ago.
When Christ conquered death as He hung on the cross,

It was then at that moment Satan knew his great loss.
He was put under Christ's feet, and he knew Christ was boss.

Restoration is coming to us down below.
Restoration's approaching earth, dying so slow.

Restoration is coming, Satan's final death blow.
Christ won the great victory, and this we should know.

Lucifer's sin didn't alter God's paradise story
Because Jesus Christ brought us to eternal glory!

August 20, 2019

# God's Love

Right from the start,
With each beat of our hearts,
God bestowed His love
From His kingdom above.
He kept an eye on us,
Protected us too,
Granted us time,
Saw us through,
Offered salvation to
Gentile and Jew,
Imparted His wisdom
And listened too,
Bestowed kindness,
Cured spiritual blindness,
Lit life with brightness,
Helped us grow,
Bestowed His grace;
Mercy overflowed.
Right from the start,
With each beat of our hearts,
God bestowed His love
From His kingdom above!

August 27, 2019

# Can You Say That for Sure?

I love people who say, "Your mom will be fine."
Not so sure they know God's will is divine.

I know they say it to make me feel better,
But don't they know health can change like the weather?

I know people care saying, "She will get better."
But existence is God's plan to the last letter.

He breathes us a soul, and we should all know
There's a time when we're born and a time we must go.

Hope I'm ready 'fore Mom's taken forever,
Called from this earth for a life that is better.


September 06, 2019

# Just Be

I won't focus on my handicaps.

God has certain assignments for me.

His grace is quite enough, I know.

It's all I'll ever really need.


I won't focus on my weaknesses;

That's when His power shows up best.

I'll finish the work He's left for me,

And then He'll call me home to rest.


September 07, 2019

# All Things Gospel

Be acutely aware of the how and the whys
Because Satan employs a duplicity of lies.
Remember first he's the master of disguise,
Opposed to God's children, desiring our demise.

In and around earth's skies, he rides;
He and demonic angels do fly,
Trying to catch us all by surprise,
To tempt weak believers to compromise,
To sit back or take flight,
To sit and not rise,
To lay back and not fight for the heavenly prize,
To give up the gospel and truths we have known,
To stay frozen in time, not spiritually grown.

So we must be grounded in all things gospel.
Rise, stand, and fight, being Christ's earthly model,
Staying always connected to the Father above,
Experiencing His forever passionate love.

As we wait for that day when we'll stand at the throne,
In that day, we will know Him as we have been known.
We'll all say goodbye to Satan's tricks and his lies,
God casting him to Hades, evil forces, and spies.
Our Lord will bind him to eternal hellfire—
The perfect end for the world's greatest liar.

September 08, 2019

# Help for Tomorrow

Don't worry 'bout tomorrow,
For God's already there.
Don't worry 'bout tomorrow;
Your future's in His care.
Don't worry 'bout tomorrow;
Just focus on today.
Don't worry 'bout tomorrow;
He'll lead you in His way.

He'll forever stand by you;
He's here always to stay,
But today, for unknown reasons,
My focus seems to stray.
It may be pure exhaustion;
My mind feels at a loss.
I know He hasn't left me,
And everything's not lost.

Grant me sleep tonight, dear Lord,
And wake me in the morn,
All refreshed to face the day,
On eagle's wings to soar.
'Cause tonight, I know You're waiting there,
Already in tomorrow.
Help me focus not so much
On tonight's tremendous sorrow.

September 12, 2019

# The Medical Center 2019
# —My September 18–29 Visit

I've been visiting every day now,
And now, just two days later,
I walk into Mom's hospital room. She says,
"I feel just so much better!"

I'm shocked to see and hear
A different woman lying there.
Her improvement happened overnight,
Coming out of nowhere!

So many questions still in my mind—
Just where all this is headed,
Envisioning and fretting.
Her death is what I'm dreading.

September 17, 2019

# Each Minute

One minute, you are fine;

The next minute, you are not.

I bet Mom never imagined

Her life would abruptly stop.

Her calendars and papers

Are strewn in rooms throughout.

I see my life a lot in hers,

And I just want to shout.

What if my path is similar?

What will I do to plan?

Yet to see a possible future

Is a blessing from His hand.

All any of us can do

Is to trust God in each minute,

Each minute that He gives us,

To live just as He sees fit!

September 18, 2019

# Raise Your Hands!

Raise your hands in praise

to the one, our Messiah Son!

He accomplished all and won.

He's not left anything undone.


Raise hands, everyone,

to the conquering king—the Son!

To the one who created all,

all creatures great and small.


Raise your hands, you lands,

up to the starry heavens!

Give glory forever and ever.

Give glory to Him. Amen.


September 19, 2019

# Time Is in God's Hand

When we must have time pass fast,

    It moves only so slow.

When we need it to slow down,

    We watch it quickly go.

But we aren't the ones deciding

    How it marches or it slows,

Whether it goes fast,

    Or where time really goes.

God's the only one

    Who decides what happens when,

And He already knows

    And has written it in pen.

Not saying we don't have choices;

    We surely make our plans.

But God's the omnipotent;

    We want our lives in His safe hand.

September 24, 2019

# Last Steps

"What is in my future, Lord?"
　　*Leave it up to Me.*
"I'm scared about Mom's future, Lord."
　　*With Me, it needs to be.*
"I was arrogant and very wrong
To think I knew all, all along.
Right now, today, I'm fifty-three.
Bearing in mind, my mom's not me—
Yet to watch her struggle hard to breathe
Is extremely hard for me to see.
I saw my dad take his last breath.
So help me, Lord, with her last steps."
　　*Your mom's future lies with Me, in heaven that's where she'll someday be.*
　　*And when your teardrops start to fall; I'll stretch My hand to catch them all.*
　　*I'll catch each one as they may come, each single tear, as I've always done.*

　　Mom passed to heaven at 9:47 p.m., October 9, 2019...


*September 25, 2019*

# The Lord Is With Us

The Lord ... guided them during the day
with a pillar of cloud,
and He provided light at night
with a pillar of fire.

This allowed them to travel by day or by night.
And the Lord did not remove the pillar of cloud
or pillar of fire
from its place in front of the people
(Exodus 13:21–22).

During daylight hours,
God guides me by the cross of His Son
using a cross-shaped utility pole the next street over
whenever I look out my kitchen window.
God provides His cross to see
just like the Israelites' pillar of cloud—
a symbol of His presence to me.

At nighttime,
God reassures me with a star
using a shining streetlight the next street over
in the same spot out my kitchen window, near the utility pole.
God provides a star to see
just like the star of Bethlehem
to comfort me.

October 14, 2019

# Victory at Calvary

You know the pain I suffer, Lord,
because You suffered too.
Your children clearly rejected You,
rejected one so true.

How did You not shed all Your tears
on the path to Calvary?
Yet when I think about it now,
not tears but blood You shed for me!

I regret it took so long, my Lord,
to give my heart to You—
the deep, true love You had for me,
but I just never knew.

October 15, 2019

# A Prayer for Jamie

You know what I am feeling, Lord,
And I heard in my heart You say to me,
"Give her to Me. Let her be.
I'll set her free."

I continued to pray: Heal her
soul, and take her pain,
And lead her as she goes,
And take my pain along with that,
And help us both to grow.

Help our aching hearts because
You have experienced it too.
And show us how to get through this,
And give us strength anew.

Today, in Jesus's name, I pray.
Thank You.

October 16, 2019

# The Great Curse/The Great Cure

God planted two trees in the middle of Eden.
They stood in the garden, put there for a reason—
To test Adam and Eve, to see if they'd listen.
The serpent twisted God's words, brazenly reasoning.
"You will not surely die, *if you eat it*," he hissed (Genesis 3:4 ESV),
Completely misleading—worked his art of deceiving.

He tricked Adam and Eve, and we paid the price—
Eternity stolen in paradise.
But under a new covenant, God's mercy was lent.
Being born into sin—now no need to repent.
Most declared God unfair because of all this;
He left us back there, cursing man, earth, and air.
But God didn't reject us because the great cure,
The cure He had planned, sits to His right hand.

In the void of time, before God created the garden,
He had the plan for eternity; He knew He'd be coming
To hang on the cross when all souls were lost.
Redemption by blood, no destruction by flood—
Just calling His name, asking forgiveness again.
No more sackcloth and ashes to repent of our sins.

The Old and New Testaments separating covenant times—
So please, no more listening to Satan's lies.
Satan's been stripped of his power, damned forever to hell.
But God knew long ago that all'd turn out well
And we'd all live together; He planned it back then
In the Garden of Eden, reestablished again!

December 25, 2019

Printed in the United States
By Bookmasters